Vorname: ______________________________

Name: ______________________________

Anschrift: ______________________________

E-Mail: ______________________________

Telefonnummer: ______________________________

Seemeilen-Nachweise vor diesem Buch

Zeitraum: ______________________________

Zurückgelegte Seemeilen: ______________________________

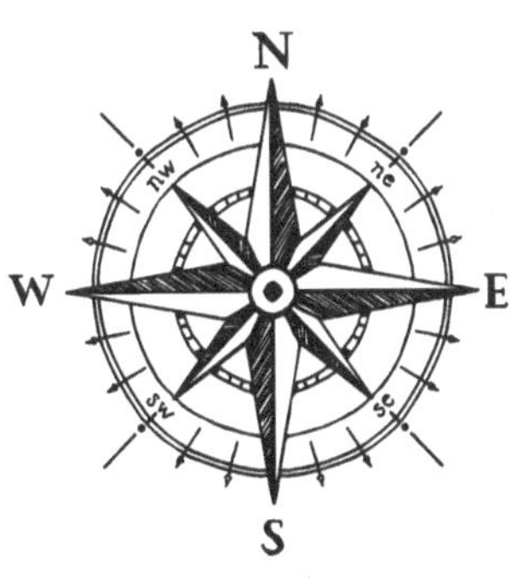

Übertrag

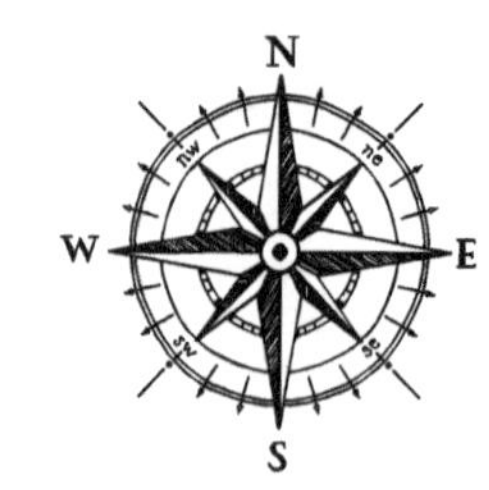

______________________ Seetage   ______________________ Seemeilen

Lfd. Nr.	Fahrgebiet / Route	Seetage	Seemeilen

Summe ______________________ ______________________

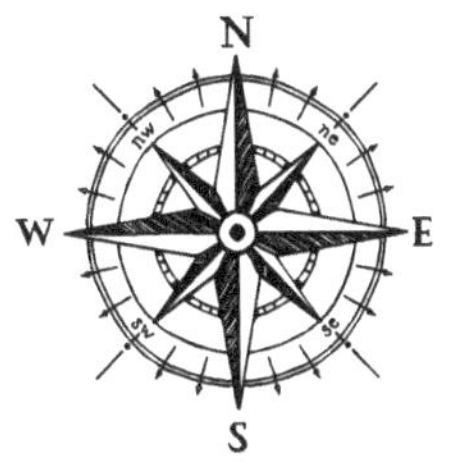

Übertrag

Seetage

Seemeilen

Lfd. Nr.	Fahrgebiet / Route	Seetage	Seemeilen

Summe ___________ ___________

Übertrag

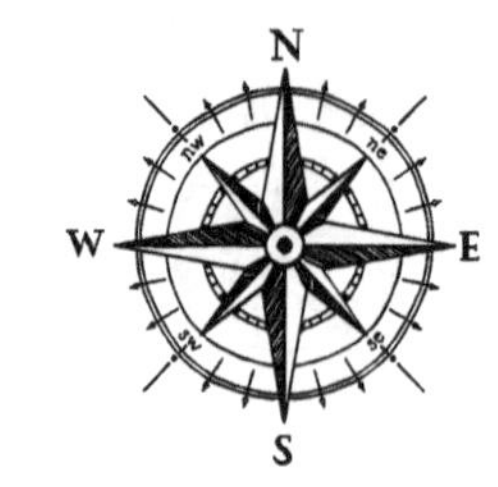

_______________ Seetage

_______________ Seemeilen

Lfd. Nr.	Fahrgebiet / Route	Seetage	Seemeilen

Summe _______________ _______________

Übertrag

________________________   ________________________
Seetage   Seemeilen

Lfd. Nr.	Fahrgebiet / Route	Seetage	Seemeilen

Summe ________________ ________________

Übertrag

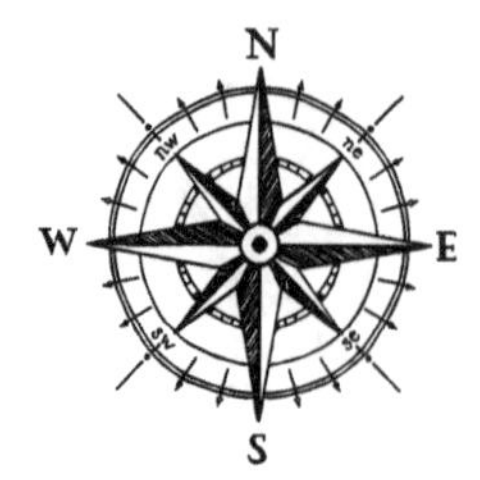

______________________ ______________________
Seetage   Seemeilen

Lfd. Nr.	Fahrgebiet / Route	Seetage	Seemeilen

Summe ______________________ ______________________

Übertrag

Seetage   **Seemeilen**

Lfd. Nr.	Fahrgebiet / Route	Seetage	Seemeilen

Summe ___________ ___________

Übertrag

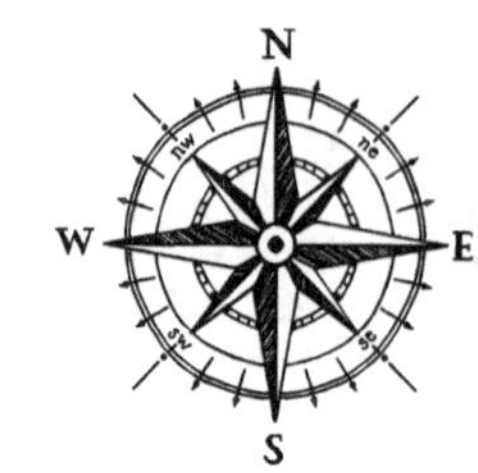

	Seetage		Seemeilen

Lfd. Nr.	Fahrgebiet / Route	Seetage	Seemeilen

Summe ______________ ________

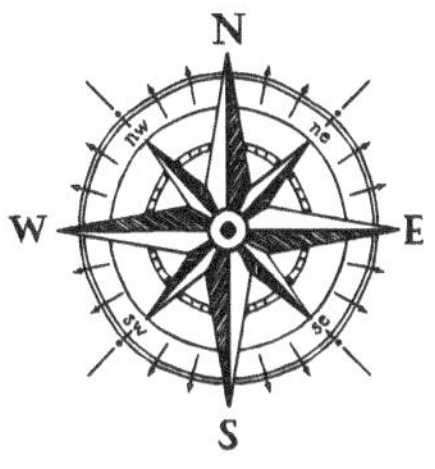

Übertrag

Seetage

Seemeilen

Lfd. Nr.	Fahrgebiet / Route	Seetage	Seemeilen

Summe ______________ ______________

Übertrag

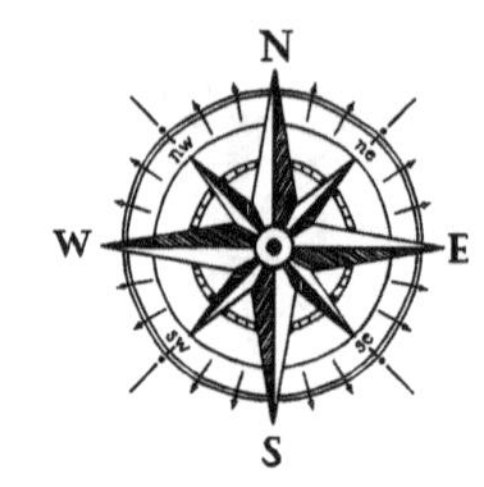

__________________ Seetage   __________________ Seemeilen

Lfd. Nr.	Fahrgebiet / Route	Seetage	Seemeilen

Summe __________________ __________________

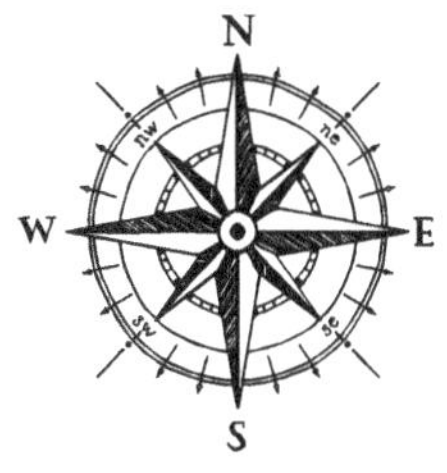

Übertrag

_________________________   _________________________

Seetage   Seemeilen

Lfd. Nr.	Fahrgebiet / Route	Seetage	Seemeilen

Summe   _________________   _________________

Übertrag

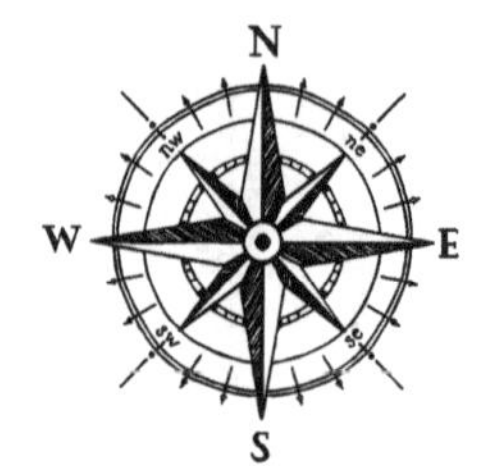

——————————————— ———————————————
Seetage   Seemeilen

Lfd. Nr.	Fahrgebiet / Route	Seetage	Seemeilen

Summe ——————————————— ———————————————

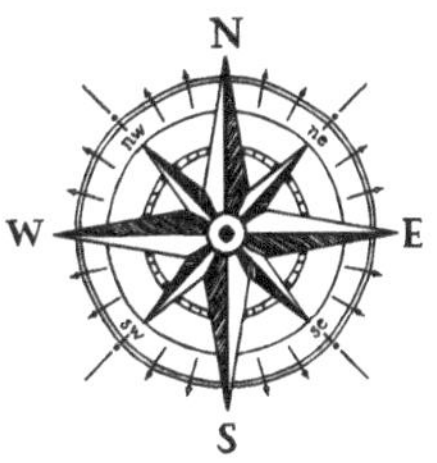

Übertrag

_______________________ _______________________
Seetage   Seemeilen

Lfd. Nr.	Fahrgebiet / Route	Seetage	Seemeilen

Summe _______________ _______________

Übertrag

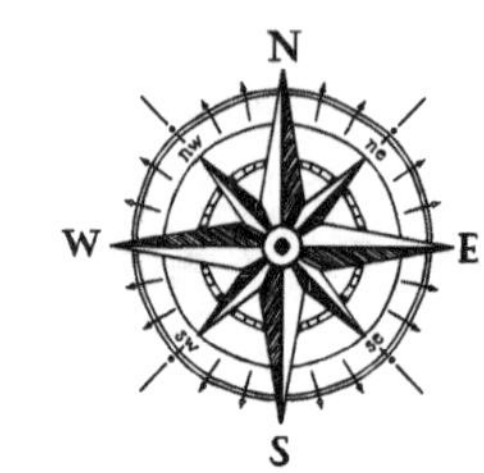

______________________   ______________________
          Seetage   **Seemeilen**

Lfd. Nr.	Fahrgebiet / Route	Seetage	Seemeilen

Summe ______________________ ______________

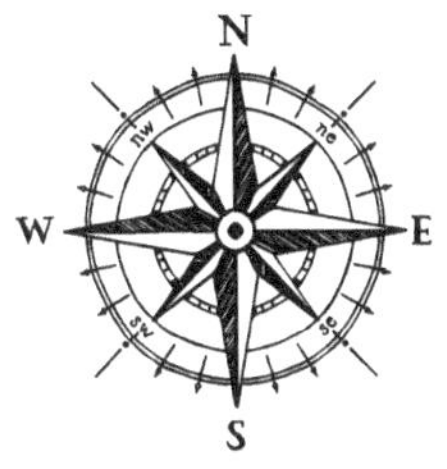

Übertrag

_________________   _________________
     Seetage   Seemeilen

Lfd. Nr.	Fahrgebiet / Route	Seetage	Seemeilen

Summe _____________ _____________

Übertrag

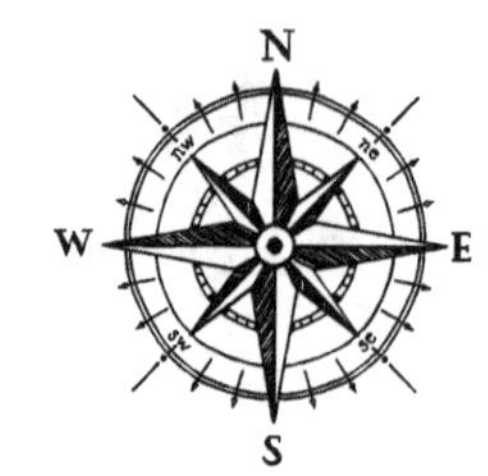

——————————————— Seetage

——————————————— Seemeilen

Lfd. Nr.	Fahrgebiet / Route	Seetage	Seemeilen

Summe ——————— ———————

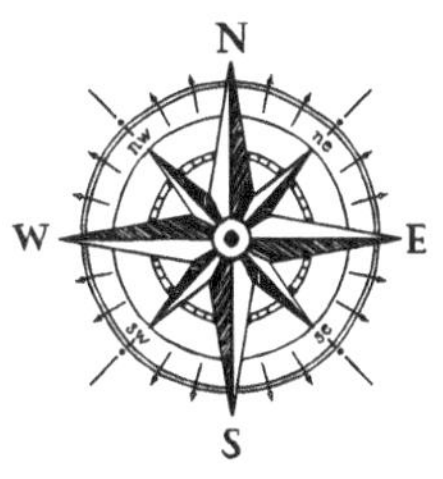

Übertrag

_________________________   _________________________

Seetage   Seemeilen

Lfd. Nr.	Fahrgebiet / Route	Seetage	Seemeilen

Summe _________________ _________________

Übertrag

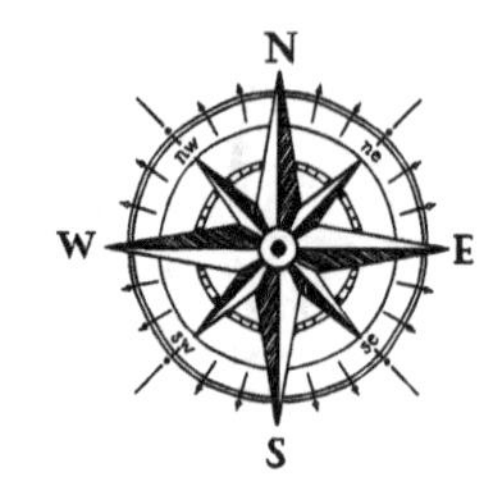

__________________ Seetage

__________________ Seemeilen

Lfd. Nr.	Fahrgebiet / Route	Seetage	Seemeilen

Summe __________ __________

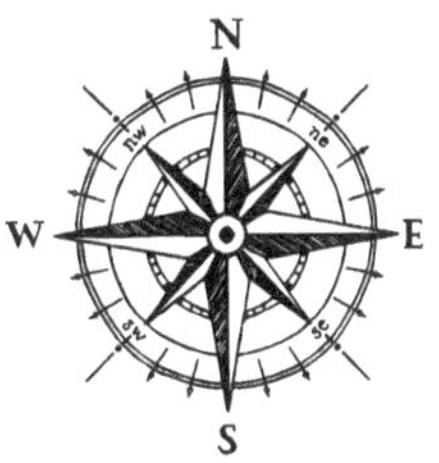

Übertrag

________________________   ________________________

Seetage   Seemeilen

Lfd. Nr.	Fahrgebiet / Route	Seetage	Seemeilen

Summe ________________   ________________

Übertrag

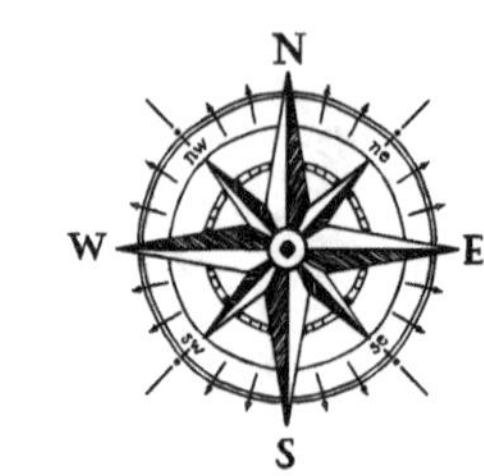

__________________ Seetage   __________________ Seemeilen

Lfd. Nr.	Fahrgebiet / Route	Seetage	Seemeilen

Summe __________________ __________________

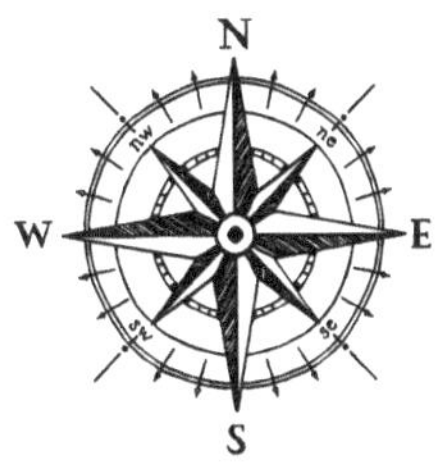

Übertrag

_____________________   _____________________

     Seetage   Seemeilen

Lfd. Nr.	Fahrgebiet / Route	Seetage	Seemeilen

Summe _____________________ _____________________

Übertrag

Seetage

Seemeilen

Lfd. Nr.	Fahrgebiet / Route	Seetage	Seemeilen

Summe

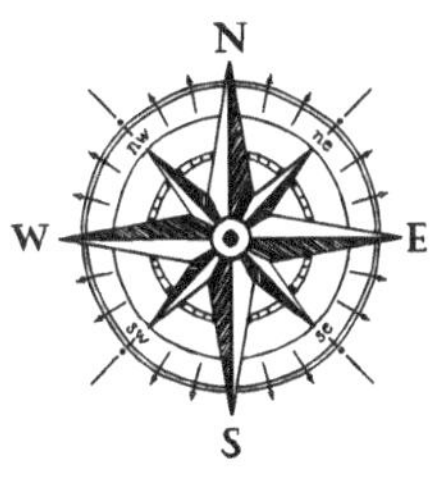

Übertrag

_______________   _______________

Seetage   Seemeilen

Lfd. Nr.	Fahrgebiet / Route	Seetage	Seemeilen

Summe _______________ _______________

Übertrag

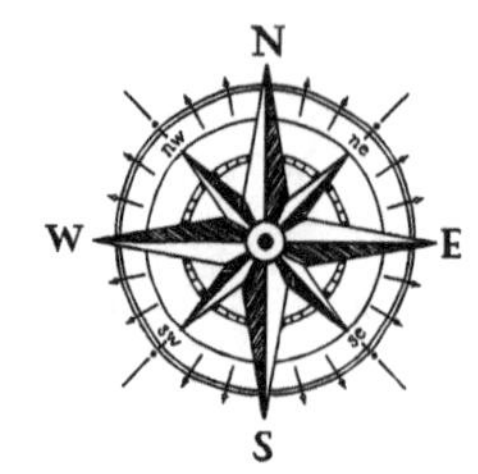

______________________ ______________________
      Seetage   Seemeilen

Lfd. Nr.	Fahrgebiet / Route	Seetage	Seemeilen

Summe ______________________ ______________________

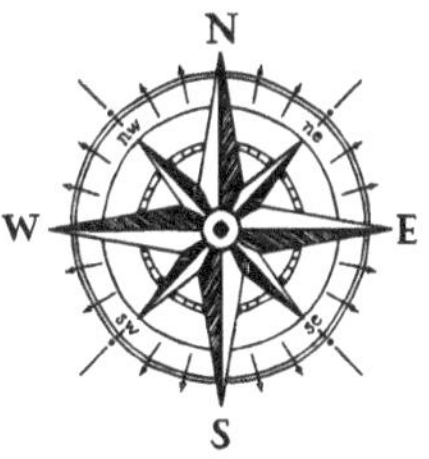

Übertrag

_______________________   _______________________

Seetage   Seemeilen

Lfd. Nr.	Fahrgebiet / Route	Seetage	Seemeilen

Summe _______________________ _______________________

Übertrag

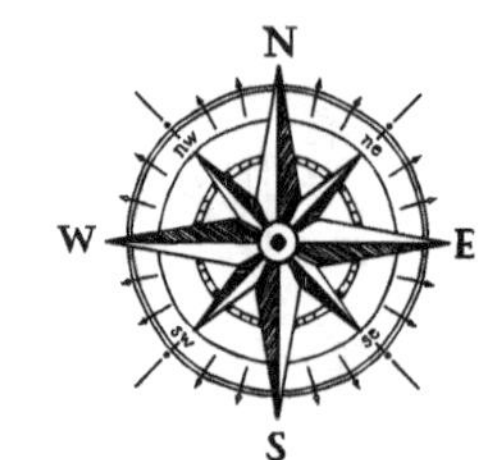

______________________   ______________________

Seetage   **Seemeilen**

Lfd. Nr.	Fahrgebiet / Route	Seetage	Seemeilen

Summe   ______________________   ______________________

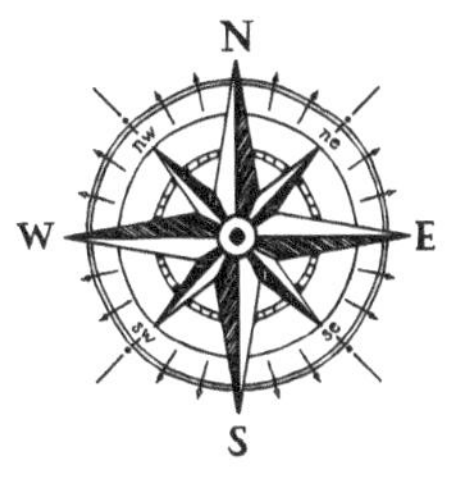

Übertrag

_______________   _______________
Seetage   **Seemeilen**

Lfd. Nr.	Fahrgebiet / Route	Seetage	Seemeilen

Summe _______________ _______________

Übertrag

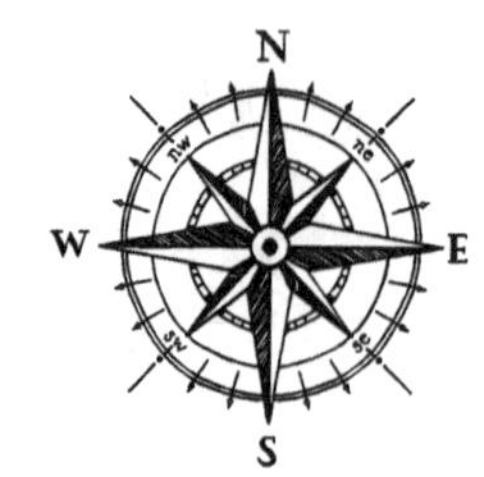

———————————— Seetage   ———————————— Seemeilen

Lfd. Nr.	Fahrgebiet / Route	Seetage	Seemeilen

Summe ———————————— ————————————

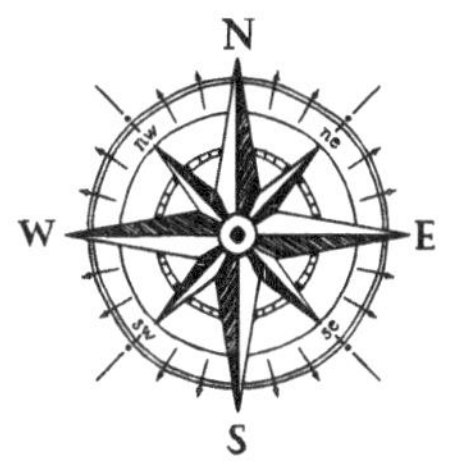

Übertrag

____
Seetage

____
Seemeilen

Lfd. Nr.	Fahrgebiet / Route	Seetage	Seemeilen

Summe _______________ _______________

Übertrag

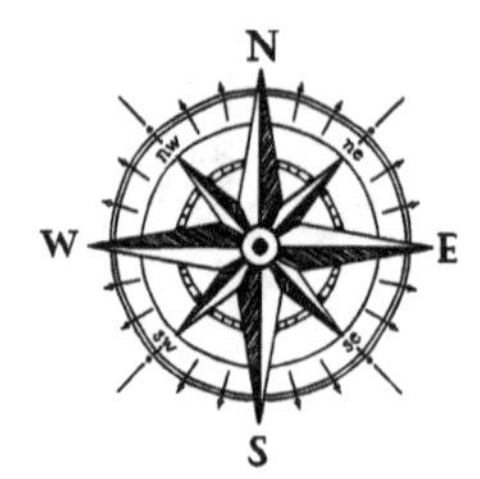

__________________________   __________________________

     Seetage   Seemeilen

Lfd. Nr.	Fahrgebiet / Route	Seetage	Seemeilen

Summe __________________________ __________________________

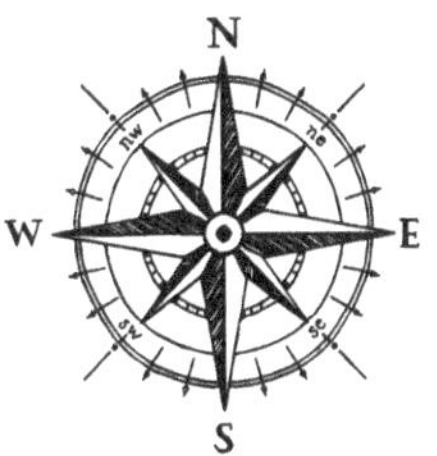

Übertrag

_______________   _______________

Seetage   Seemeilen

Lfd. Nr.	Fahrgebiet / Route	Seetage	Seemeilen

Summe _______________ _______________

Übertrag

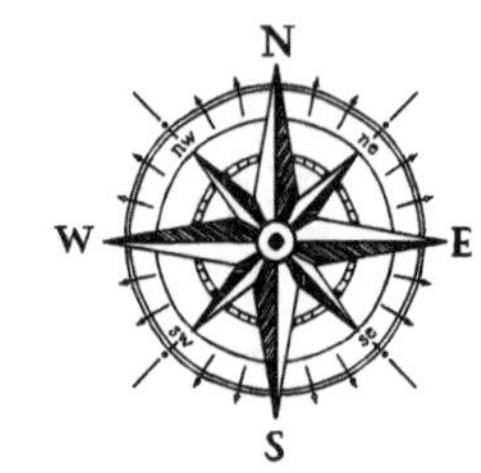

______________________   ______________________

       Seetage   **Seemeilen**

Lfd. Nr.	Fahrgebiet / Route	Seetage	Seemeilen

Summe ______________   ______________

Übertrag

__________________________   __________________________

Seetage   Seemeilen

Lfd. Nr.	Fahrgebiet / Route	Seetage	Seemeilen

Summe __________________________   __________________________

Übertrag

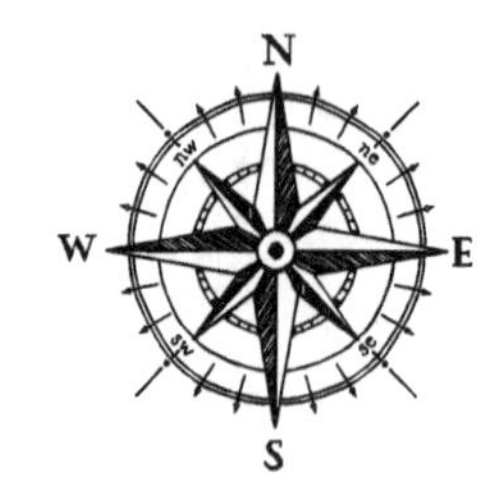

__________________________   __________________________

      Seetage   **Seemeilen**

Lfd. Nr.	Fahrgebiet / Route	Seetage	Seemeilen

Summe __________________ __________________

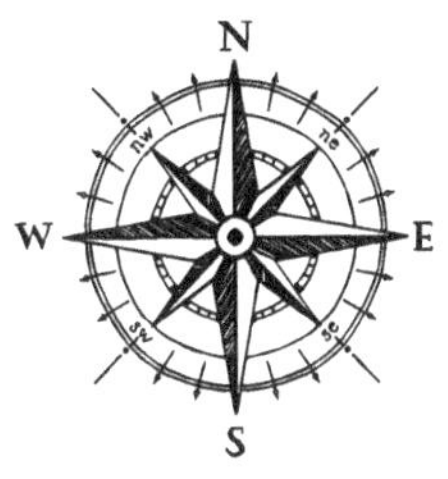

Übertrag

____________________   ____________________

Seetage   Seemeilen

Lfd. Nr.	Fahrgebiet / Route	Seetage	Seemeilen

Summe ____________________ ____________________

Übertrag

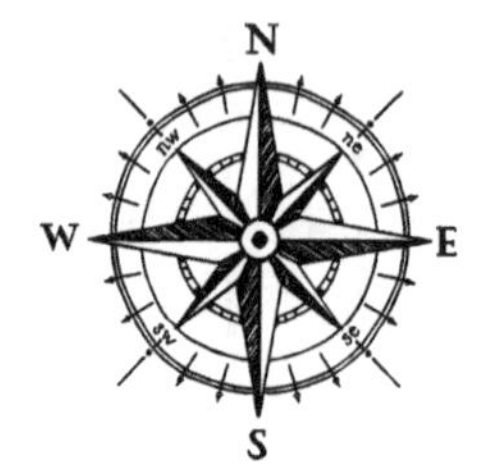

___________________   ___________________

        Seetage   **Seemeilen**

Lfd. Nr.	Fahrgebiet / Route	Seetage	Seemeilen

Summe   ___________________   ___________________

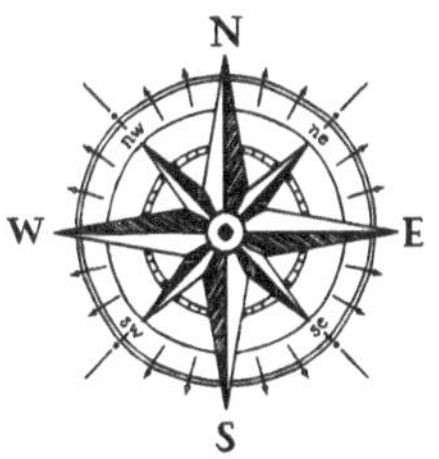

Übertrag

____
Seetage

____
Seemeilen

Lfd. Nr.	Fahrgebiet / Route	Seetage	Seemeilen

Summe _______________ _______________

Übertrag

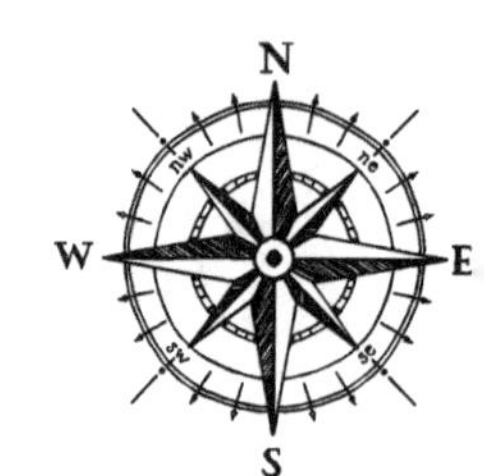

__________________ Seetage

__________________ Seemeilen

Lfd. Nr.	Fahrgebiet / Route	Seetage	Seemeilen

Summe __________________ __________________

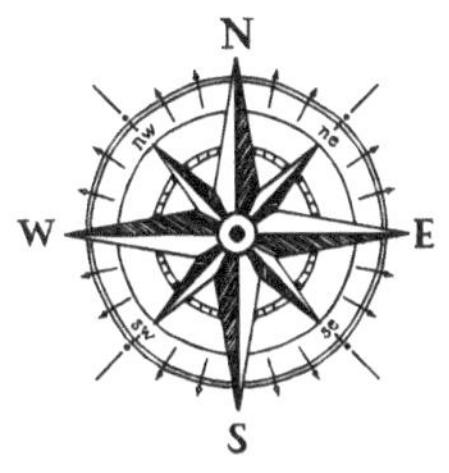

Übertrag

______________________   ______________________
Seetage   Seemeilen

Lfd. Nr.	Fahrgebiet / Route	Seetage	Seemeilen

Summe ______________________ ______________________

Übertrag

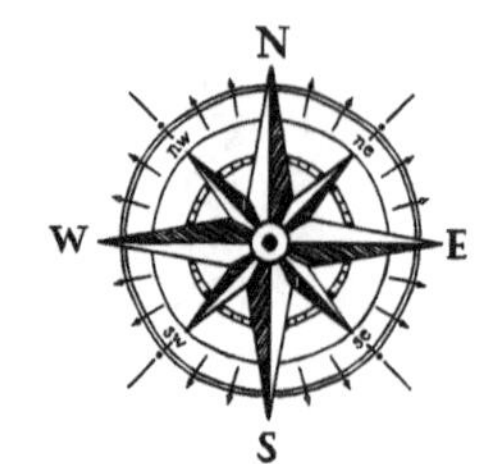

Seetage   **Seemeilen**

Lfd. Nr.	Fahrgebiet / Route	Seetage	Seemeilen

Summe ______________ ______________

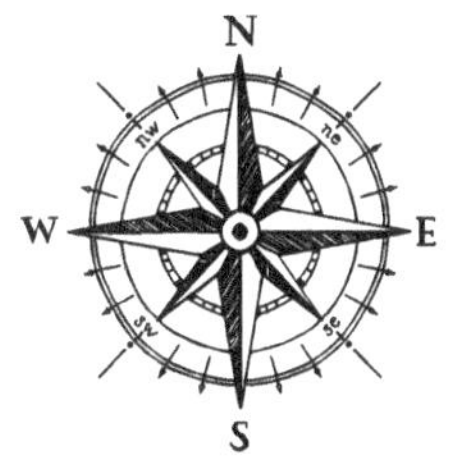

Übertrag

______________________   ______________________
Seetage   Seemeilen

Lfd. Nr.	Fahrgebiet / Route	Seetage	Seemeilen

Summe ______________   ______________

Übertrag

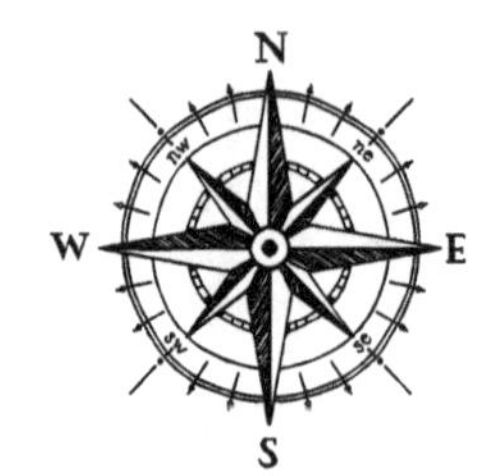

_______________________   _______________________

Seetage   **Seemeilen**

Lfd. Nr.	Fahrgebiet / Route	Seetage	Seemeilen

Summe _______________________ _______________________

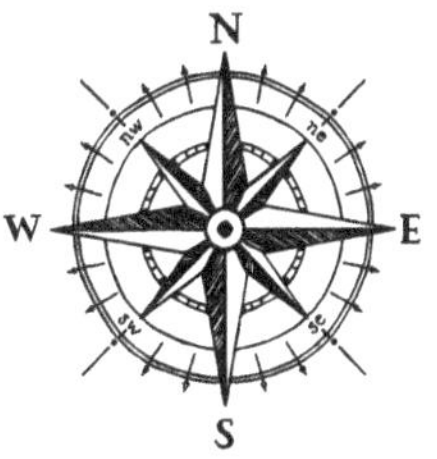

Übertrag

——————————— ———————————
Seetage   Seemeilen

Lfd. Nr.	Fahrgebiet / Route	Seetage	Seemeilen

Summe ——————————— ———————————

Übertrag

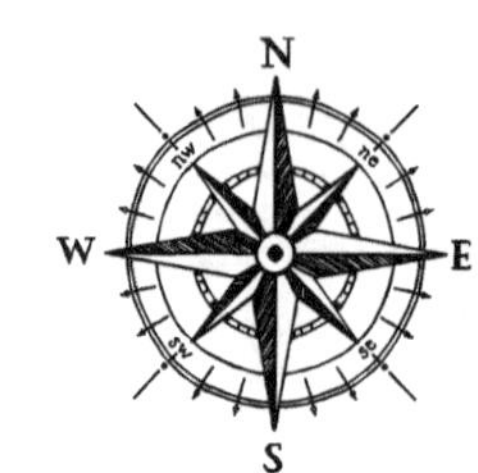

Seetage   **Seemeilen**

Lfd. Nr.	Fahrgebiet / Route	Seetage	Seemeilen

Summe _______ _______

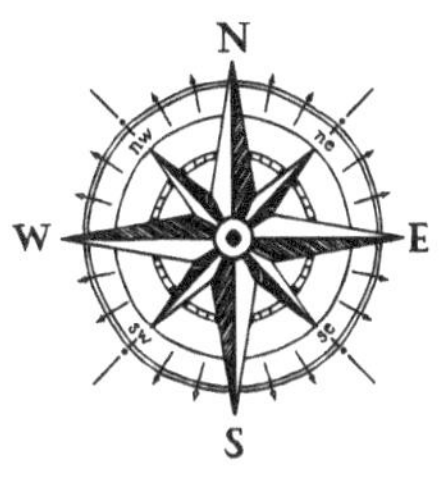

Übertrag

_______________   _______________

Seetage   Seemeilen

Lfd. Nr.	Fahrgebiet / Route	Seetage	Seemeilen

Summe _______________ _______________

Übertrag

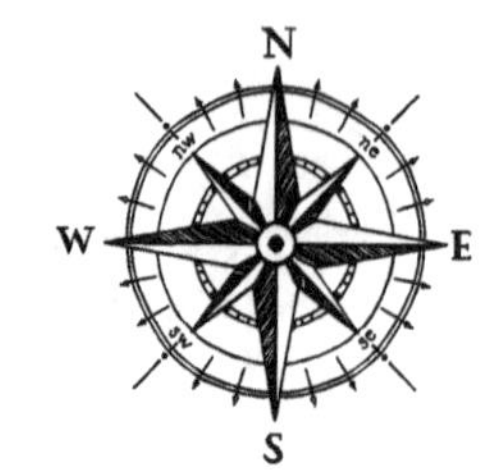

__________________________   __________________________

         Seetage   Seemeilen

Lfd. Nr.	Fahrgebiet / Route	Seetage	Seemeilen

Summe   __________________   __________________

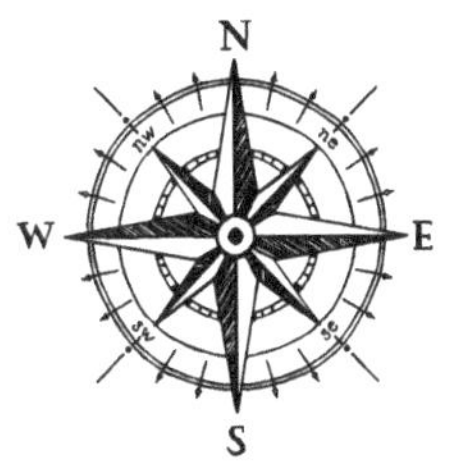

Übertrag

__________________________   __________________________

Seetage   Seemeilen

Lfd. Nr.	Fahrgebiet / Route	Seetage	Seemeilen

Summe __________________ __________________

Übertrag

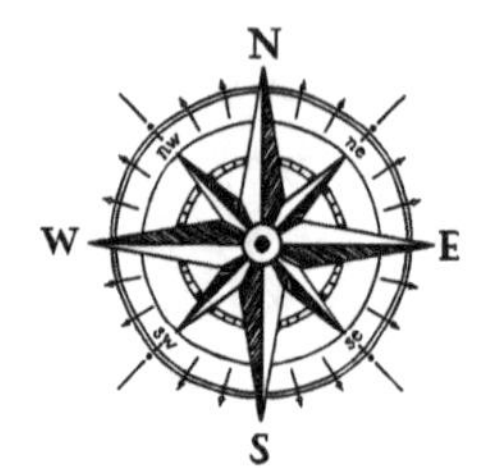

__________________ Seetage

__________________ Seemeilen

Lfd. Nr.	Fahrgebiet / Route	Seetage	Seemeilen

Summe __________________ __________________

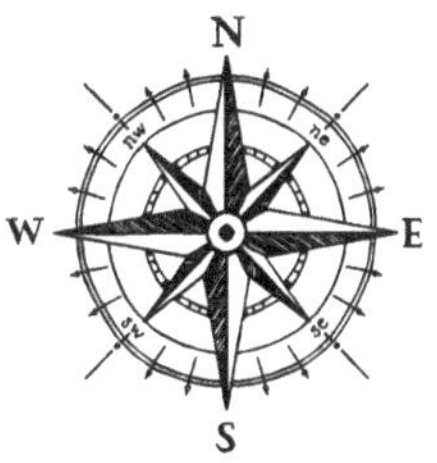

Übertrag

____
Seetage

____
Seemeilen

Lfd. Nr.	Fahrgebiet / Route	Seetage	Seemeilen

Summe _______________ _______________

Übertrag

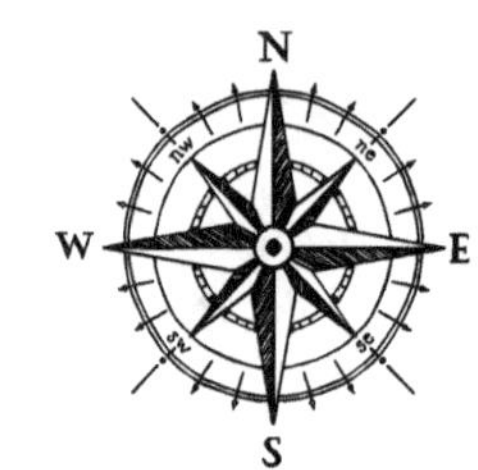

____________________ ____________________
Seetage   Seemeilen

Lfd. Nr.	Fahrgebiet / Route	Seetage	Seemeilen

Summe ____________________ ____________________

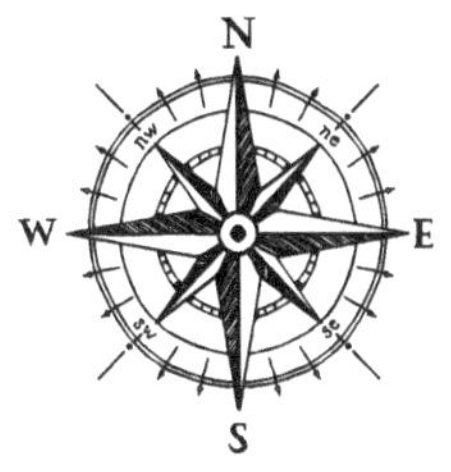

Übertrag

_____________________   _____________________

Seetage   Seemeilen

Lfd. Nr.	Fahrgebiet / Route	Seetage	Seemeilen

Summe _____________________ _____________________

Übertrag

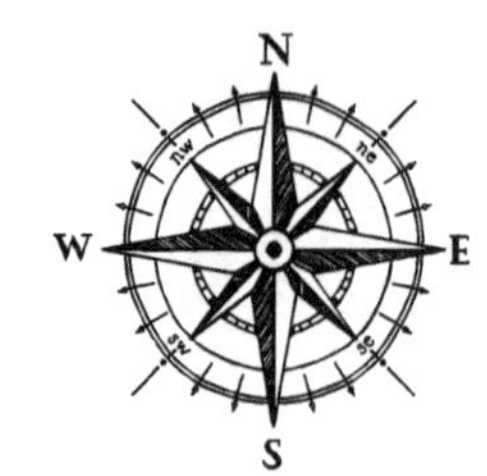

___________________   ___________________
Seetage   Seemeilen

Lfd. Nr.	Fahrgebiet / Route	Seetage	Seemeilen

Summe ___________________ ___________________

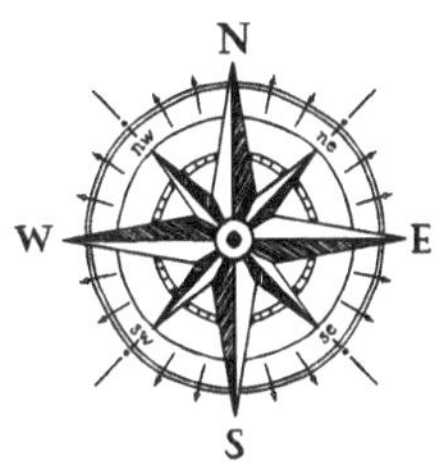

Übertrag

_______________________   _______________________

Seetage   Seemeilen

Lfd. Nr.	Fahrgebiet / Route	Seetage	Seemeilen

Summe   _______________   _______________

Übertrag

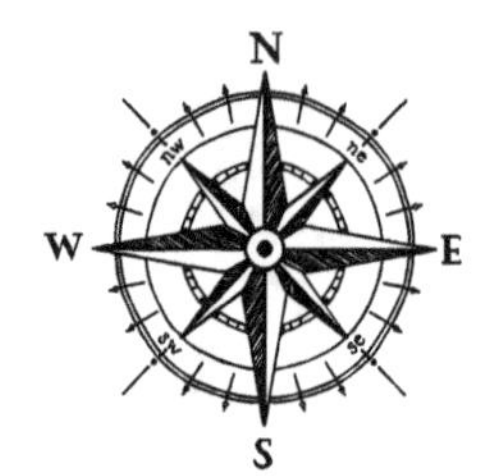

______________________   ______________________

Seetage   **Seemeilen**

Lfd. Nr.	Fahrgebiet / Route	Seetage	Seemeilen

Summe   ______________   ______________

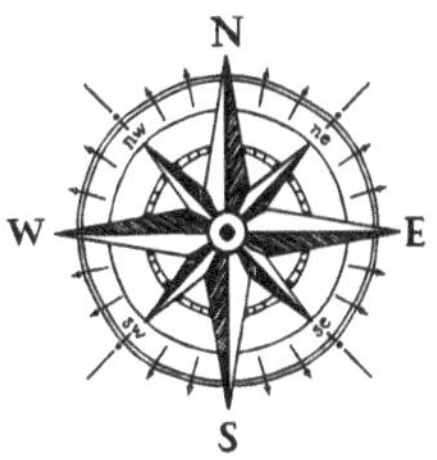

Übertrag

_______________   _______________

Seetage   Seemeilen

Lfd. Nr.	Fahrgebiet / Route	Seetage	Seemeilen

Summe _______________   _______________

Übertrag

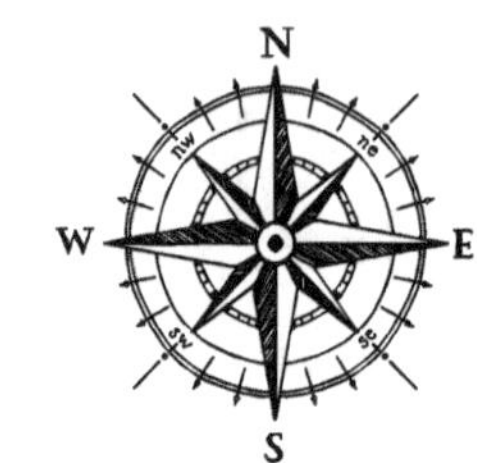

__________________ Seetage

__________________ Seemeilen

Lfd. Nr.	Fahrgebiet / Route	Seetage	Seemeilen

Summe __________________ __________________

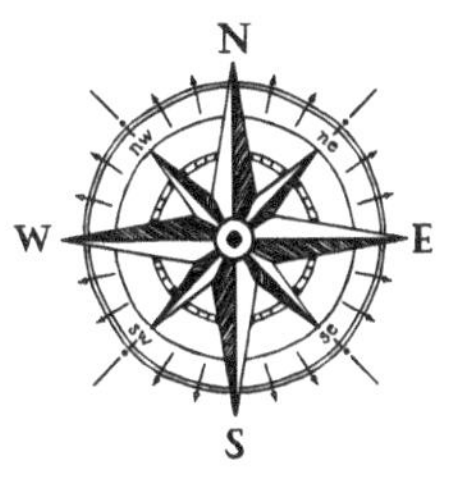

Übertrag

_______________   _______________

Seetage   Seemeilen

Lfd. Nr.	Fahrgebiet / Route	Seetage	Seemeilen

Summe   _______________   _______________

Übertrag

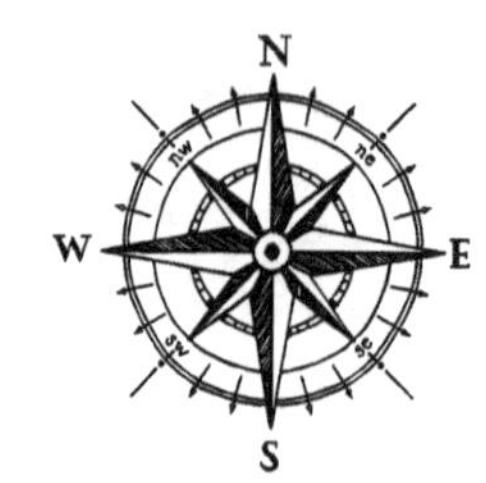

Seetage

Seemeilen

Lfd. Nr.	Fahrgebiet / Route	Seetage	Seemeilen

Summe ______________ ______________

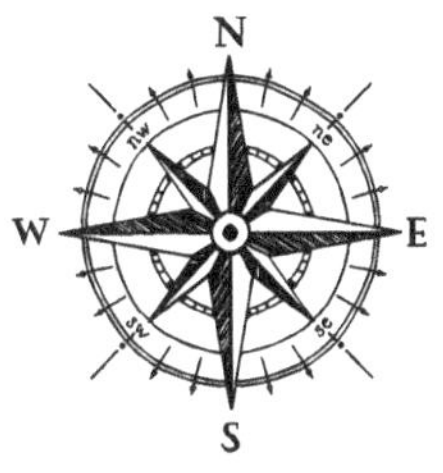

Übertrag

_________________________   _________________________

Seetage   Seemeilen

Lfd. Nr.	Fahrgebiet / Route	Seetage	Seemeilen

Summe _________________ _________________

Übertrag

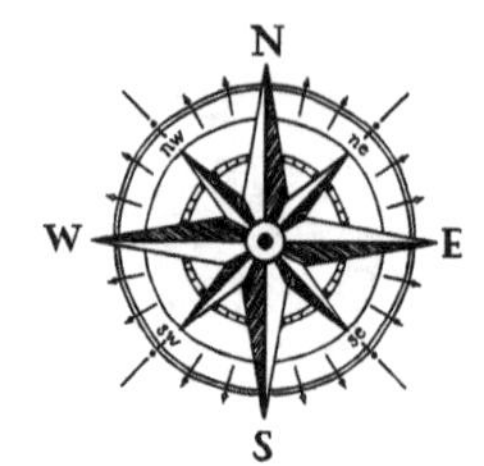

______________________   ______________________

Seetage   **Seemeilen**

Lfd. Nr.	Fahrgebiet / Route	Seetage	Seemeilen

Summe ______________________   ______________________

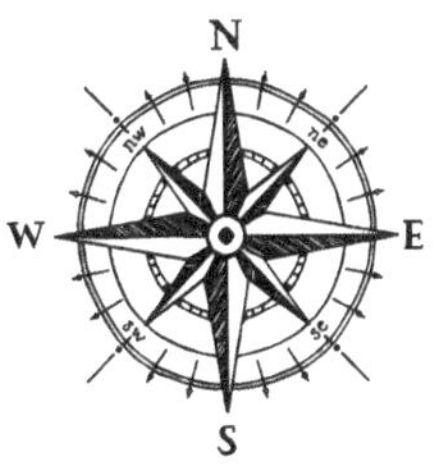

Übertrag

__________________   __________________

Seetage   Seemeilen

Lfd. Nr.	Fahrgebiet / Route	Seetage	Seemeilen

Summe __________________   __________________

Übertrag

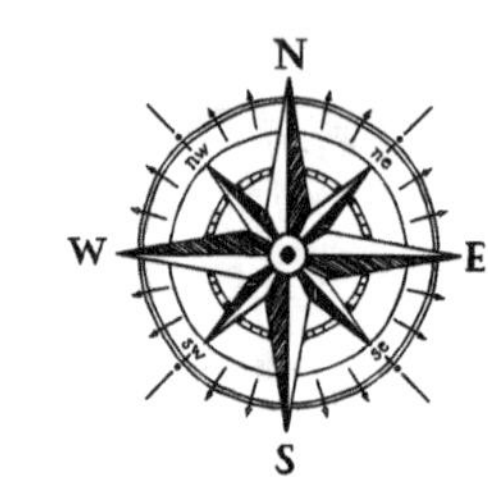

______________________   ______________________
Seetage   Seemeilen

Lfd. Nr.	Fahrgebiet / Route	Seetage	Seemeilen

Summe ______________________   ______________________

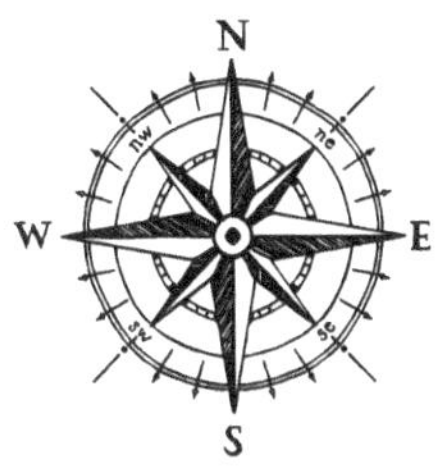

Übertrag

_______________________   _______________________

Seetage   Seemeilen

Lfd. Nr.	Fahrgebiet / Route	Seetage	Seemeilen

Summe _______________ _______________

Übertrag

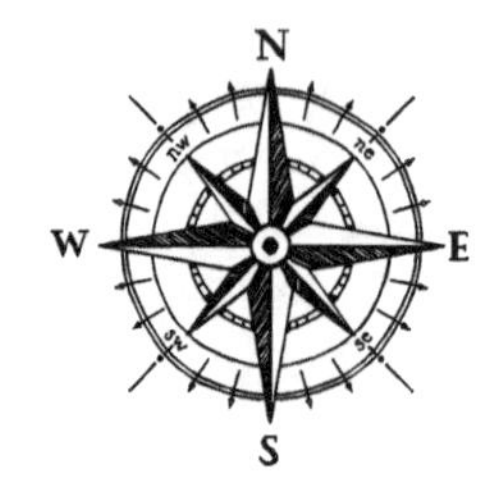

______________________ ______________________
Seetage   Seemeilen

Lfd. Nr.	Fahrgebiet / Route	Seetage	Seemeilen

Summe ______________________ ______________________

Übertrag

_______________   _______________

Seetage   Seemeilen

Lfd. Nr.	Fahrgebiet / Route	Seetage	Seemeilen

Summe   _______________   _______________

Übertrag

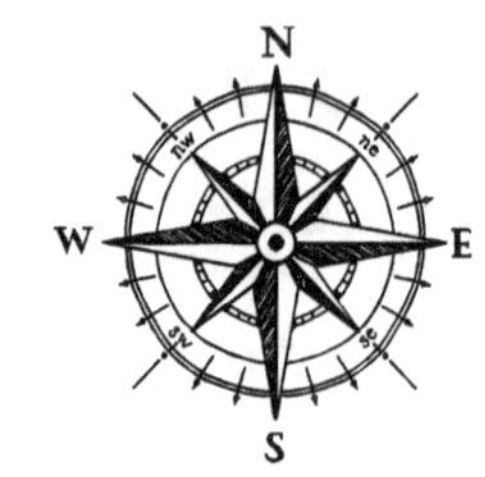

______________________   ______________________

Seetage   **Seemeilen**

Lfd. Nr.	Fahrgebiet / Route	Seetage	Seemeilen

Summe ______________________   ______________________

Übertrag

_____________________   _____________________

Seetage   Seemeilen

Lfd. Nr.	Fahrgebiet / Route	Seetage	Seemeilen

Summe   _____________________   _____________________

Übertrag

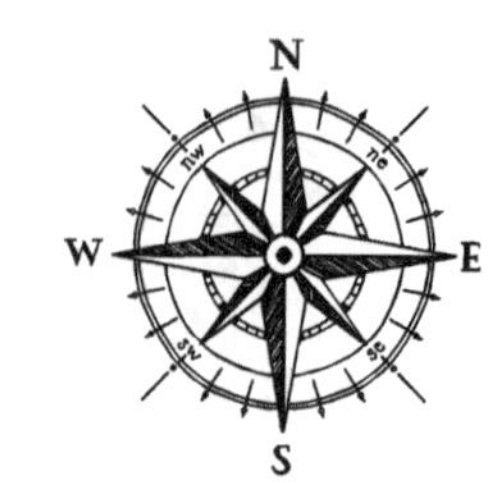

__________________ Seetage

__________________ Seemeilen

Lfd. Nr.	Fahrgebiet / Route	Seetage	Seemeilen

Summe __________________ __________________

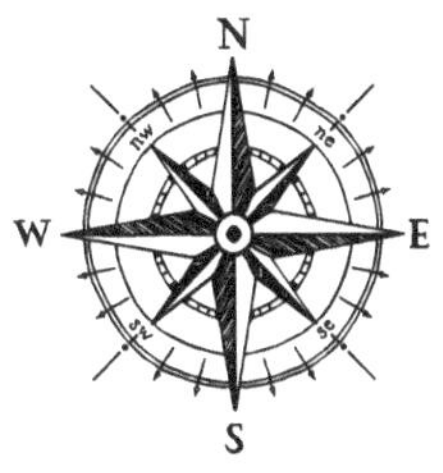

Übertrag

______________________   ______________________

Seetage   Seemeilen

Lfd. Nr.	Fahrgebiet / Route	Seetage	Seemeilen

Summe ______________ ______________

Übertrag

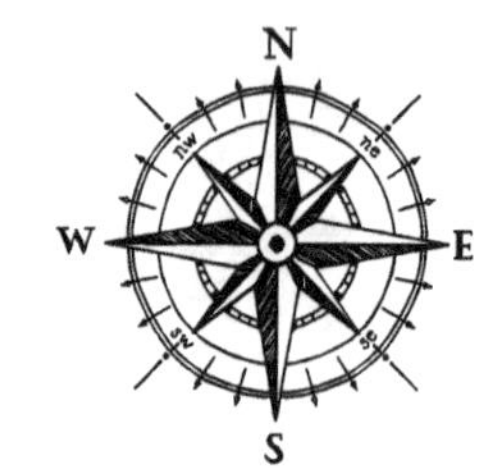

__________________   __________________
        Seetage   Seemeilen

Lfd. Nr.	Fahrgebiet / Route	Seetage	Seemeilen

Summe __________________ __________________

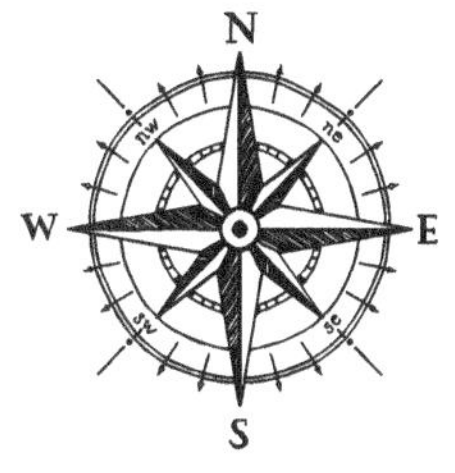

Übertrag

_______________ Seetage

_______________ Seemeilen

Lfd. Nr.	Fahrgebiet / Route	Seetage	Seemeilen

Summe _______________ _______________

Übertrag

__________________ __________________
Seetage   Seemeilen

Lfd. Nr.	Fahrgebiet / Route	Seetage	Seemeilen

Summe __________________ __________________

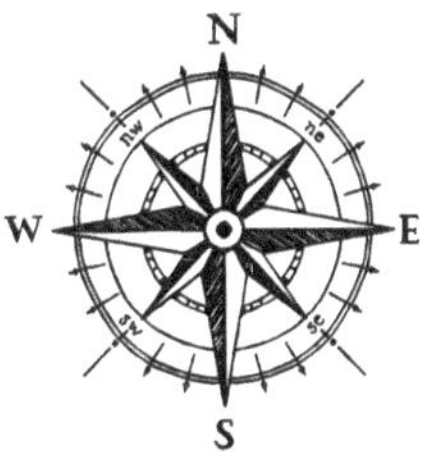

Übertrag

——————————————— ———————————————
Seetage   Seemeilen

Lfd. Nr.	Fahrgebiet / Route	Seetage	Seemeilen

Summe ——————————— ———————————

Übertrag

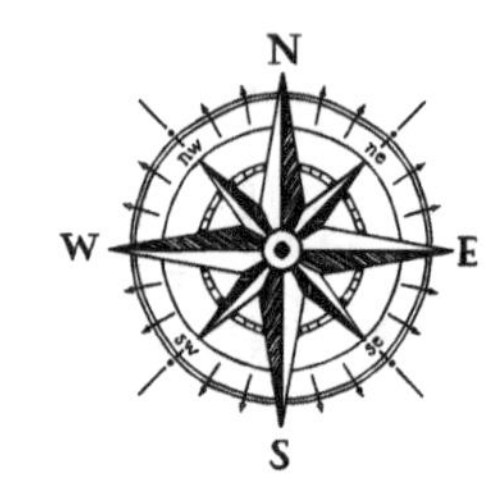

______________________   ______________________
        Seetage   Seemeilen

Lfd. Nr.	Fahrgebiet / Route	Seetage	Seemeilen

Summe ______________________

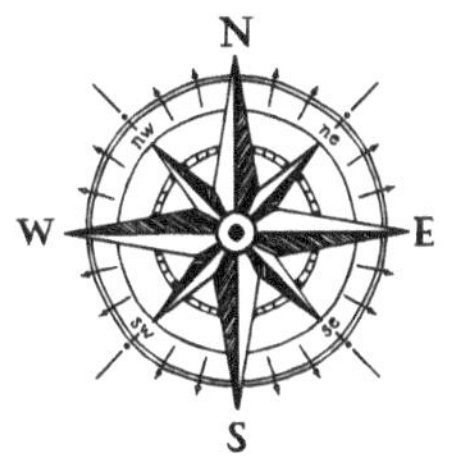

Übertrag

______________________   ______________________

Seetage   Seemeilen

Lfd. Nr.	Fahrgebiet / Route	Seetage	Seemeilen

Summe   ______________ ______________

Übertrag

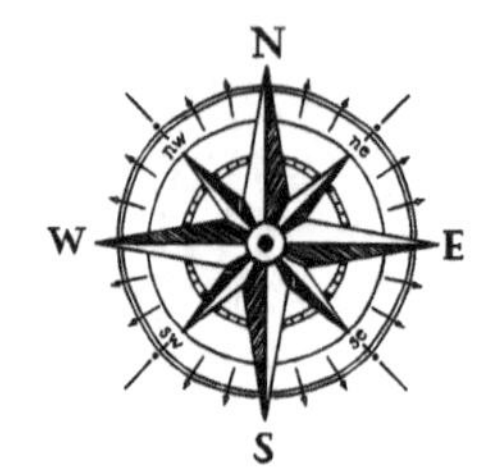

____________________   ____________________
        Seetage   Seemeilen

Lfd. Nr.	Fahrgebiet / Route	Seetage	Seemeilen

Summe   ____________________   ____________________

Übertrag

__________________   __________________

     Seetage   Seemeilen

Lfd. Nr.	Fahrgebiet / Route	Seetage	Seemeilen

Summe __________________ __________________

Übertrag

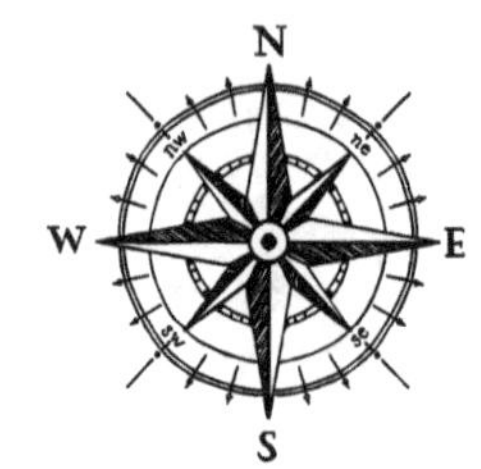

_______________   _______________
Seetage   **Seemeilen**

Lfd. Nr.	Fahrgebiet / Route	Seetage	Seemeilen

Summe _______________ _______________

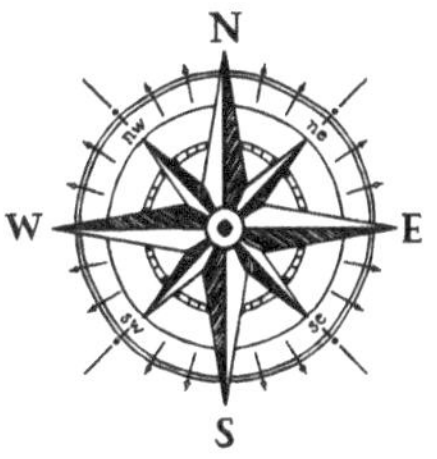

Übertrag

————————————   ————————————
Seetage   Seemeilen

Lfd. Nr.	Fahrgebiet / Route	Seetage	Seemeilen

Summe ———————————— ————————————

Übertrag

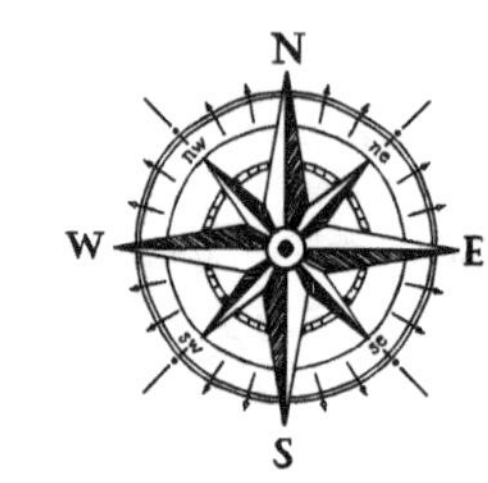

_____________________   _____________________
Seetage   **Seemeilen**

Lfd. Nr.	Fahrgebiet / Route	Seetage	Seemeilen

Summe _____________ _____________

Übertrag

____
Seetage

____
Seemeilen

Lfd. Nr.	Fahrgebiet / Route	Seetage	Seemeilen

Summe _______________ _______________

Übertrag

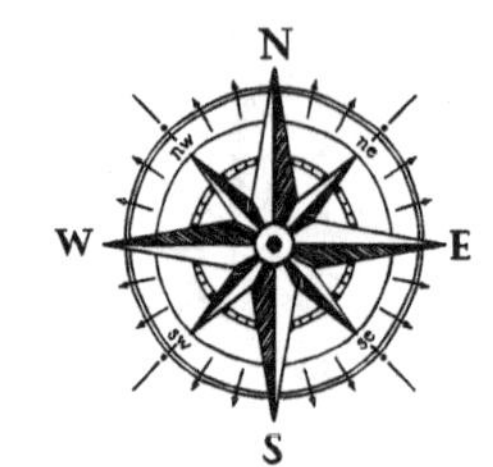

_______________ Seetage   _______________ Seemeilen

Lfd. Nr.	Fahrgebiet / Route	Seetage	Seemeilen

Summe _______________ _______________

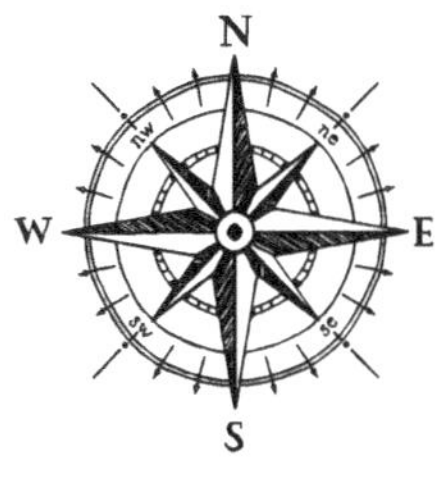

Übertrag

____
Seetage

____
Seemeilen

Lfd. Nr.	Fahrgebiet / Route	Seetage	Seemeilen

Summe ___________ ___________

Übertrag

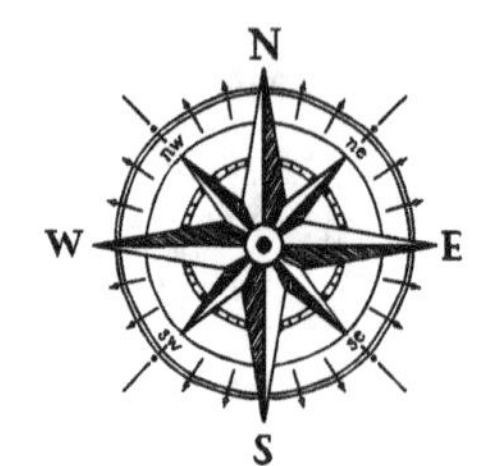

__________________ Seetage   __________________ Seemeilen

Lfd. Nr.	Fahrgebiet / Route	Seetage	Seemeilen

Summe __________________ __________________

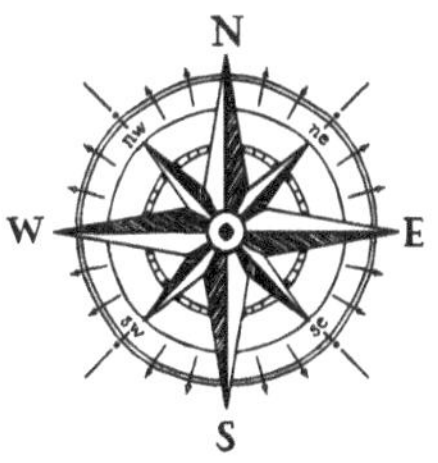

Übertrag

Seetage		**Seemeilen**

Lfd. Nr.	Fahrgebiet / Route	Seetage	Seemeilen

Summe

Übertrag

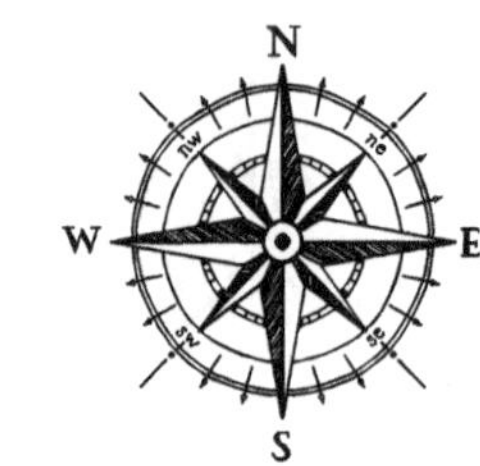

_________________________   _________________________
Seetage   Seemeilen

Lfd. Nr.	Fahrgebiet / Route	Seetage	Seemeilen

Summe _________________ _________________

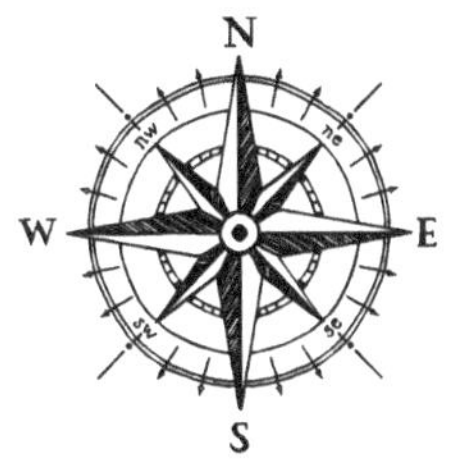

Übertrag

____
Seetage

____
Seemeilen

Lfd. Nr.	Fahrgebiet / Route	Seetage	Seemeilen

Summe _______________ _______________

Übertrag

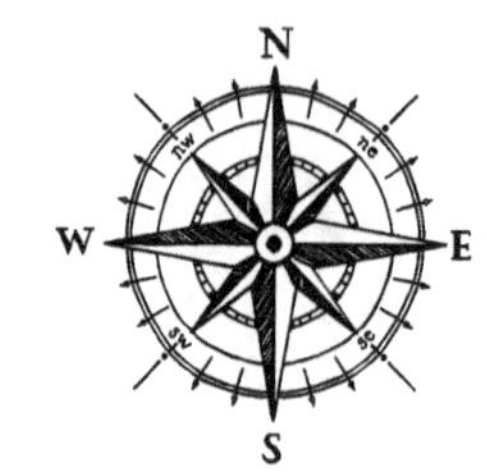

__________________ Seetage __________________ Seemeilen

Lfd. Nr.	Fahrgebiet / Route	Seetage	Seemeilen

Summe __________________ __________________

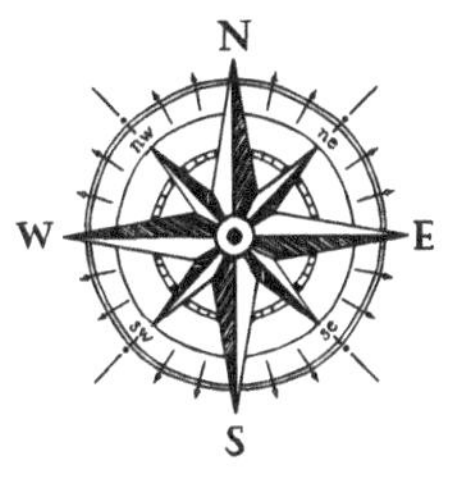

Übertrag

_________________ Seetage

_________________ Seemeilen

Lfd. Nr.	Fahrgebiet / Route	Seetage	Seemeilen

Summe _____________ _____________

Übertrag

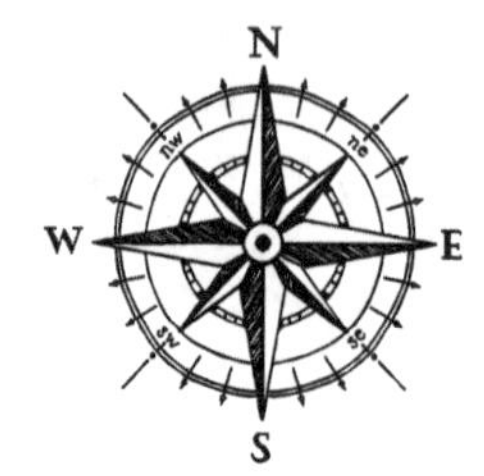

Seetage

Seemeilen

Lfd. Nr.	Fahrgebiet / Route	Seetage	Seemeilen

Summe _______________ ________

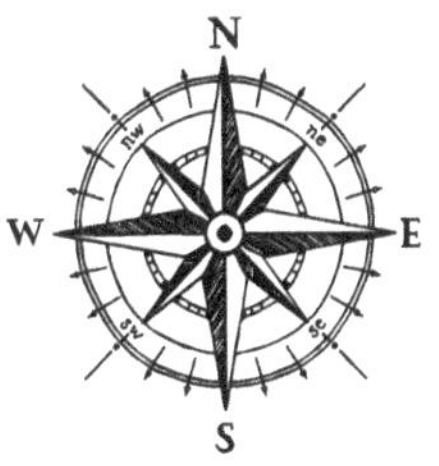

Übertrag

__________________________ __________________________
Seetage   Seemeilen

Lfd. Nr.	Fahrgebiet / Route	Seetage	Seemeilen

Summe __________________ __________________

Übertrag

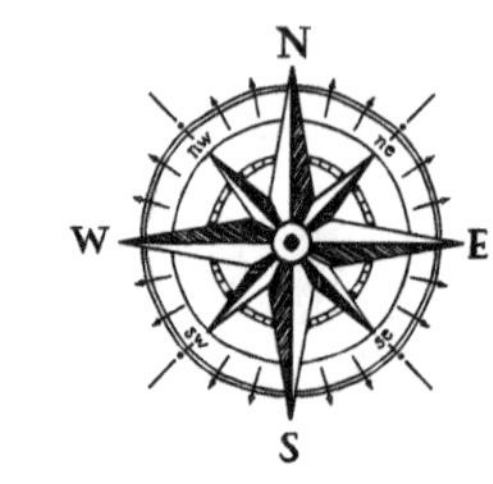

Seetage

Seemeilen

Lfd. Nr.	Fahrgebiet / Route	Seetage	Seemeilen

Summe _______________ _______________

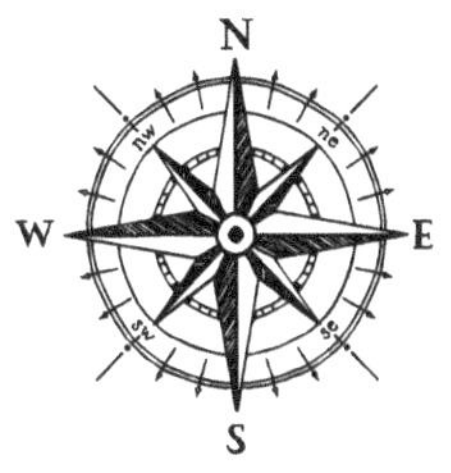

Übertrag

___________________   ___________________
Seetage   Seemeilen

Lfd. Nr.	Fahrgebiet / Route	Seetage	Seemeilen

Summe   ___________________   ___________________

Übertrag

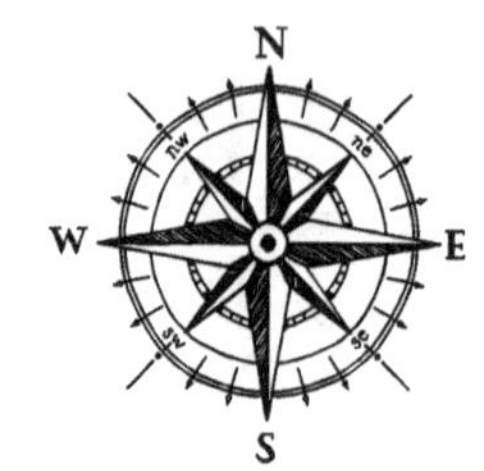

__________________ Seetage   __________________ Seemeilen

Lfd. Nr.	Fahrgebiet / Route	Seetage	Seemeilen

Summe __________________ __________________

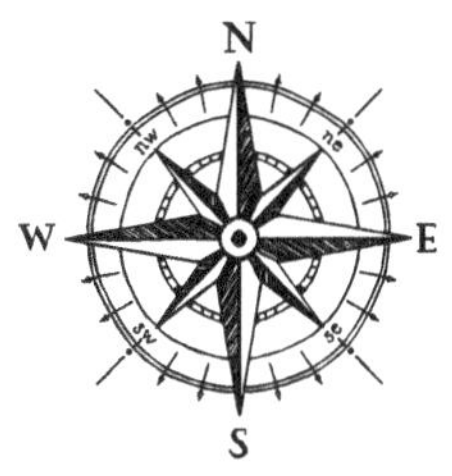

Übertrag

____
Seetage

____
Seemeilen

Lfd. Nr.	Fahrgebiet / Route	Seetage	Seemeilen

Summe __________ __________

Übertrag

______________________   ______________________

Seetage   **Seemeilen**

Lfd. Nr.	Fahrgebiet / Route	Seetage	Seemeilen

Summe   ______________________   ______________________

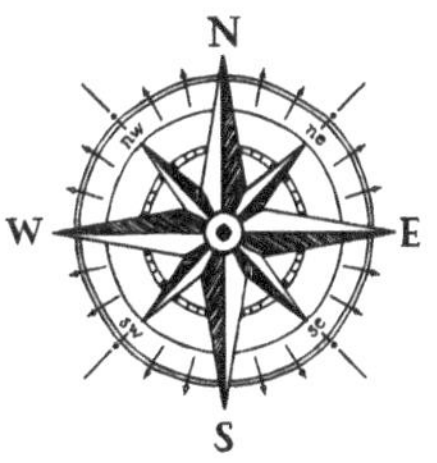

Übertrag

_______________   _______________
Seetage   Seemeilen

Lfd. Nr.	Fahrgebiet / Route	Seetage	Seemeilen

Summe _______________ _______________

Übertrag

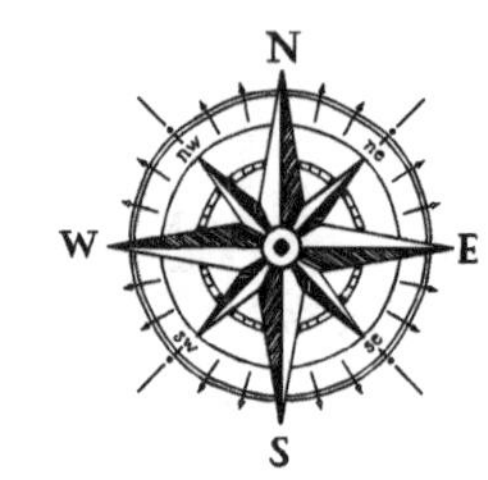

______________________   ______________________

         Seetage   **Seemeilen**

Lfd. Nr.	Fahrgebiet / Route	Seetage	Seemeilen

Summe ______________ ______

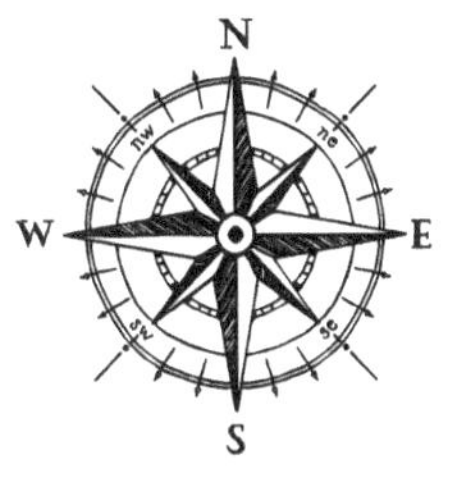

Übertrag

_______________   _______________

Seetage   Seemeilen

Lfd. Nr.	Fahrgebiet / Route	Seetage	Seemeilen

Summe _______________ _______________

Übertrag

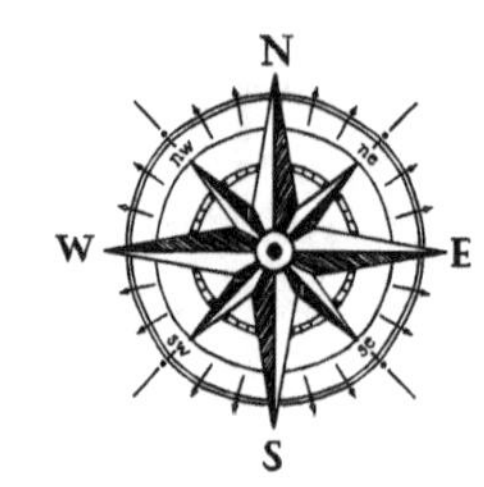

_________________	_________________
Seetage	Seemeilen

Lfd. Nr.	Fahrgebiet / Route	Seetage	Seemeilen

Summe _________________ _________________

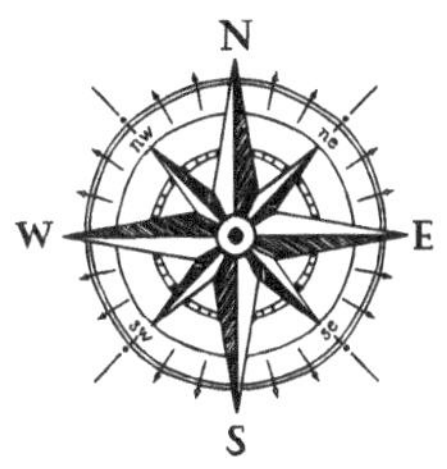

Übertrag

____
Seetage

____
Seemeilen

Lfd. Nr.	Fahrgebiet / Route	Seetage	Seemeilen

Summe _______________ _______________

Übertrag

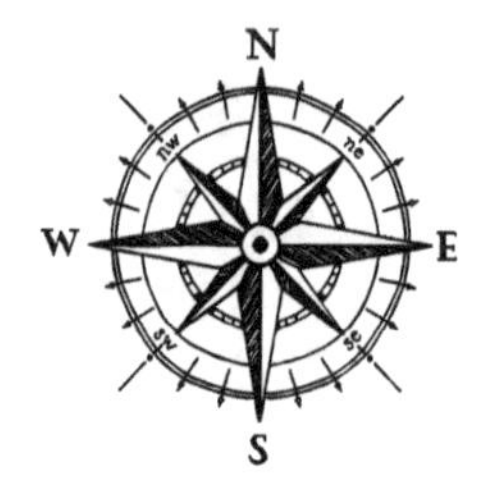

_________________________   _________________________

Seetage   Seemeilen

Lfd. Nr.	Fahrgebiet / Route	Seetage	Seemeilen

Summe _________________ _________________

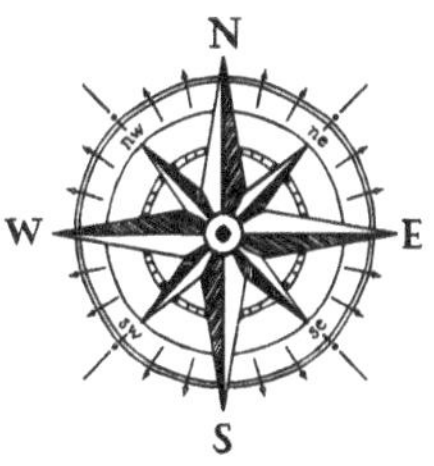

Übertrag

__________________ __________________
Seetage   Seemeilen

Lfd. Nr.	Fahrgebiet / Route	Seetage	Seemeilen

Summe __________________ __________________

Übertrag

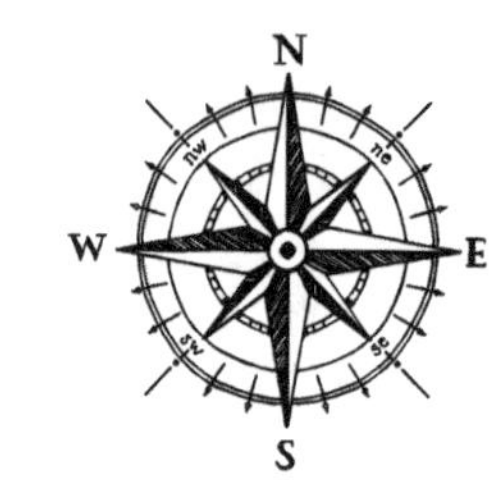

__________________ Seetage   __________________ Seemeilen

Lfd. Nr.	Fahrgebiet / Route	Seetage	Seemeilen

Summe ___________________ ___________________

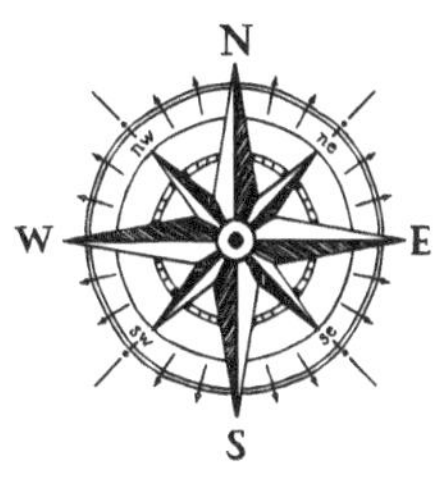

Übertrag

__________________________ __________________________
Seetage   Seemeilen

Lfd. Nr.	Fahrgebiet / Route	Seetage	Seemeilen

Summe __________________ __________________

Übertrag

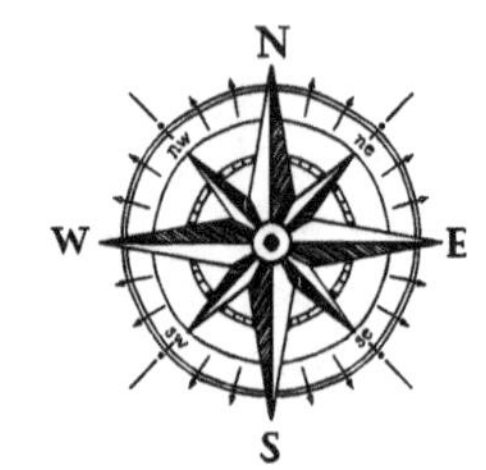

_______________   _______________

Seetage   Seemeilen

Lfd. Nr.	Fahrgebiet / Route	Seetage	Seemeilen

Summe _______________ _______________

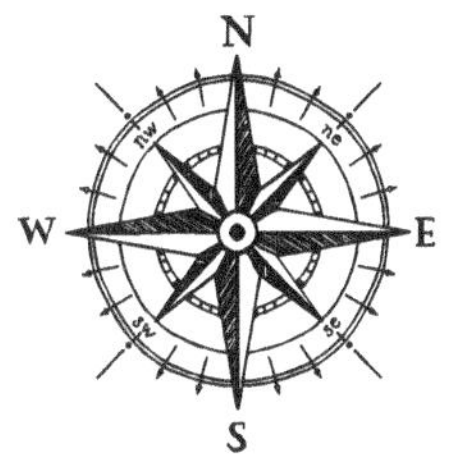

Übertrag

____
Seetage

____
Seemeilen

Lfd. Nr.	Fahrgebiet / Route	Seetage	Seemeilen

Summe _______________ _______________

Übertrag

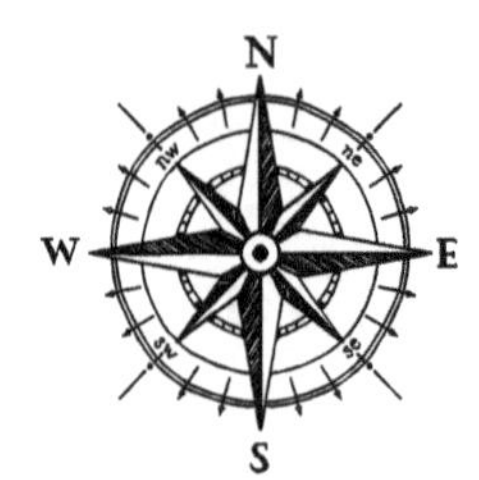

__________________   __________________
Seetage   Seemeilen

Lfd. Nr.	Fahrgebiet / Route	Seetage	Seemeilen

Summe __________________   __________________

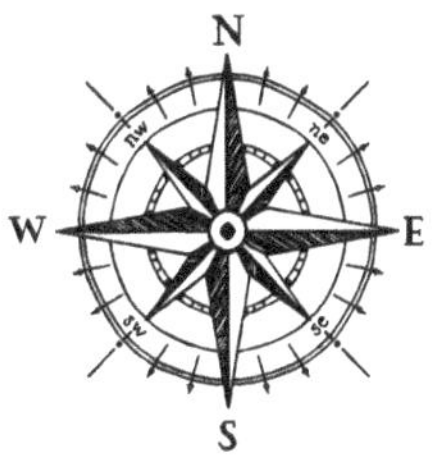

Übertrag

_______________________   _______________________

      Seetage   Seemeilen

Lfd. Nr.	Fahrgebiet / Route	Seetage	Seemeilen

Summe _______________ _______________

Übertrag

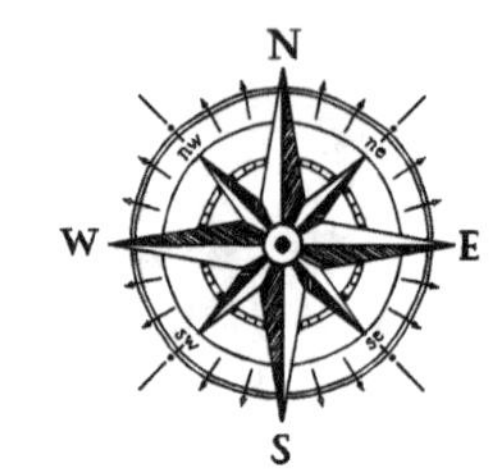

	Seetage		Seemeilen

Lfd. Nr.	Fahrgebiet / Route	Seetage	Seemeilen

Summe

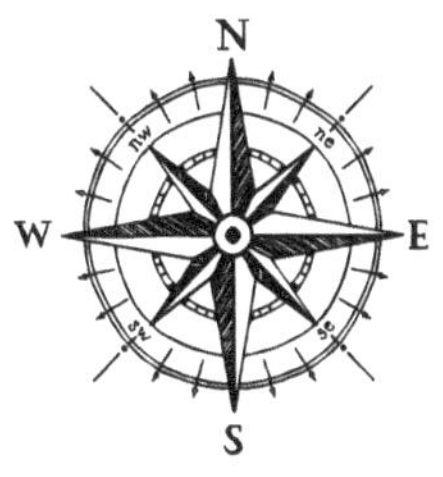

Übertrag

_________________ Seetage

_________________ Seemeilen

Lfd. Nr.	Fahrgebiet / Route	Seetage	Seemeilen

Summe _________________ _________________

Übertrag

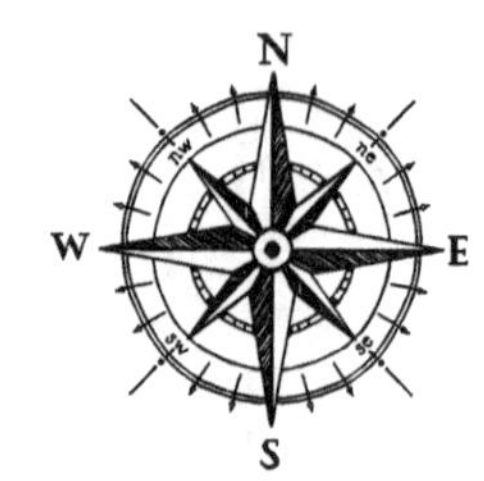

__________________ **Seetage**   __________________ **Seemeilen**

Lfd. Nr.	Fahrgebiet / Route	Seetage	Seemeilen

Summe __________________ __________________

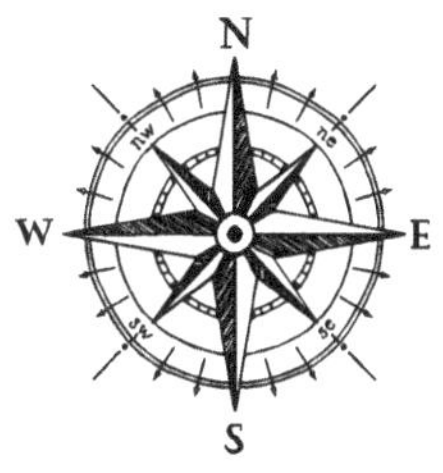

Übertrag

_______________   _______________
Seetage   Seemeilen

Lfd. Nr.	Fahrgebiet / Route	Seetage	Seemeilen

Summe _______________ _______________

Übertrag

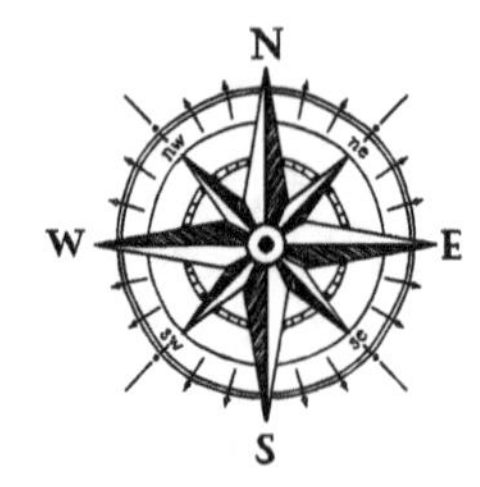

__________________ Seetage   __________________ Seemeilen

Lfd. Nr.	Fahrgebiet / Route	Seetage	Seemeilen

Summe __________________ __________________

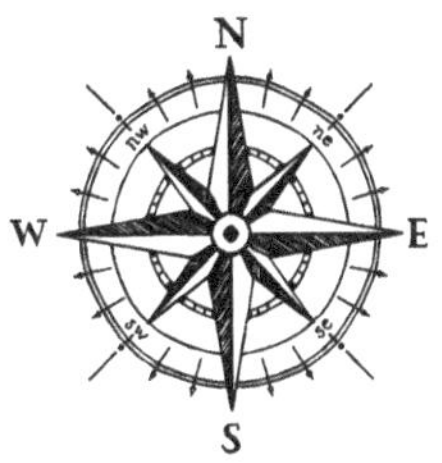

Übertrag

____________________   ____________________

Seetage   Seemeilen

Lfd. Nr.	Fahrgebiet / Route	Seetage	Seemeilen

Summe ____________ ____________

Übertrag

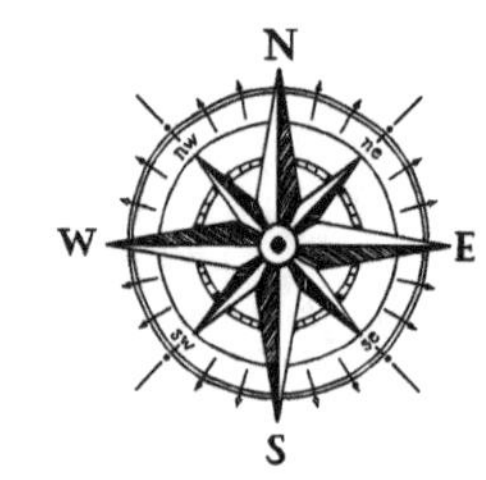

_______________________   _______________________
        Seetage   Seemeilen

Lfd. Nr.	Fahrgebiet / Route	Seetage	Seemeilen

Summe _______________ _______________

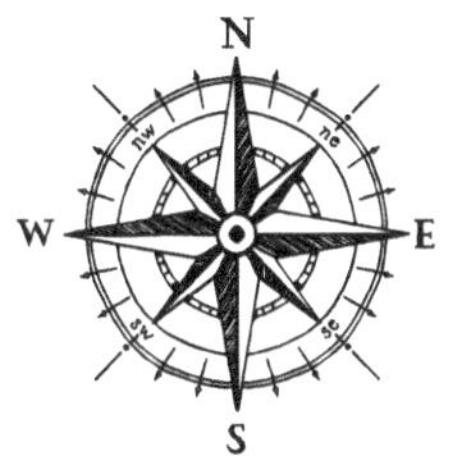

Übertrag

____
Seetage

____
Seemeilen

Lfd. Nr.	Fahrgebiet / Route	Seetage	Seemeilen

Summe _______________ _______________

Übertrag

__________________ Seetage

__________________ Seemeilen

Lfd. Nr.	Fahrgebiet / Route	Seetage	Seemeilen

Summe __________ __________

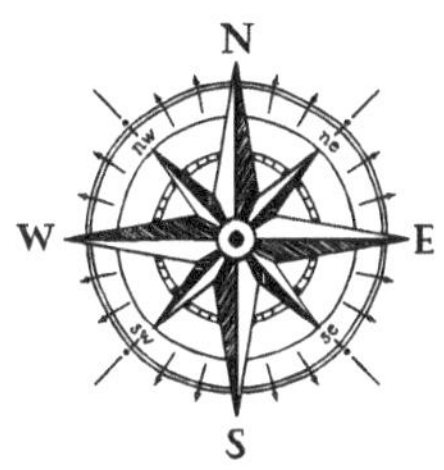

Übertrag

_______________________   _______________________

Seetage   Seemeilen

Lfd. Nr.	Fahrgebiet / Route	Seetage	Seemeilen

Summe _______________ _______________

Übertrag

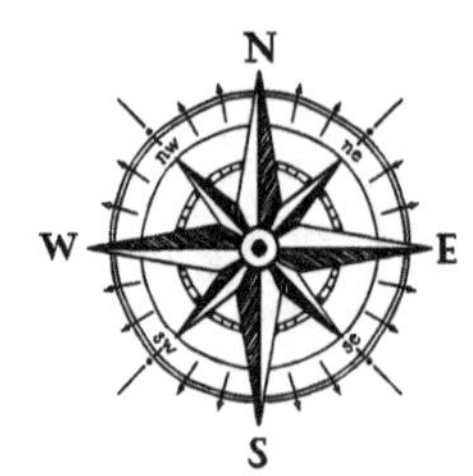

__________________   __________________
Seetage   Seemeilen

Lfd. Nr.	Fahrgebiet / Route	Seetage	Seemeilen

Summe __________________ __________________